Key Element Guide
Service Strategy

London: TSO

information & publishing solutions

Published by TSO (The Stationery Office) and available from:

Online
www.tsoshop.co.uk

Mail, Telephone, Fax & E-mail
TSO
PO Box 29, Norwich NR3 1GN
Telephone orders/General enquiries: 0870 600 5522
Fax orders: 0870 600 5533
E-mail: customer.services@tso.co.uk
Textphone: 0870 240 3701

TSO Shops
16 Arthur Street, Belfast BT1 4GD
028 9023 8451 Fax 028 9023 5401
71 Lothian Road, Edinburgh EH3 9AZ
0870 606 5566 Fax 0870 606 5588

TSO@Blackwell and other Accredited Agents

First published 2008

ISBN 9780113310708 (Sold in a pack of 10 copies)
ISBN 9780113311194 (Single copy ISBN)

Printed in the United Kingdom for The Stationery Office
N5769857   03/08

Contents

Acknowledgements

ITIL AUTHORING TEAM

- Sharon Taylor (Aspect Group Inc)   Chief Architect
- Damian Harris (Accenture)   Author
- Majid Iqbal (Gartner)   Author
- Michael Nieves (Accenture)   Author
- Ryan Thomas (Accenture)   Author

REVIEWERS

OGC would like to recognize the contribution of the following individuals:

Peter Brooks, John Groom, Matiss Horodishtiano, Kirstie Magowan and Dean Taylor

and from *it*SMF's International Publications Executive Sub-Committee (IPESC):

Matiss Horodishtiano (Lead Assessor), Marianna Billington (NZ), Bart van Brabant (Belgium), Jenny Ellwood-Wade (NZ), Robert Falkowitz (Switzerland), Juan Jose Figueriras (Argentina), Ashley Hanna (UK), Sergio Hrabinski (Argentina), Dalibor Petrovic (Canada), David Salischiker (Argentina) and Robert Stroud (US).

1 Introduction

This publication is intended to provide a synopsis of the basic concepts and practice elements of Service Strategy, which forms part of the core ITIL Service Management Practices. These practices form the ITIL Service Lifecycle on which the concepts of these and all other ITIL Service Management publications are based.

This publication is not intended to replace the ITIL core publications and should not be used in place of the full practice guidance publications. The content in this publication is depicted at a high level and will not be practical as a substitute for the full guidance publication; rather it should serve as a handy quick reference that is portable and helps direct the reader to the full guidance information when needed.

1.1   THE ITIL FRAMEWORK

ITIL Service Management has been practised successfully around the world for more than 20 years. Over this time, the framework has evolved from a specialized set of service management topics with a focus on function to a process-based framework and now to a broader, holistic service lifecycle. The evolution and transformation of ITIL Service Management Practices is the result of the evolution of the IT service management (ITSM) industry itself, through knowledge, experience, technical innovation and thought leadership. The ITIL Service Lifecycle is both a reflection of the industry practice in use today, and concepts that will move us forward in the future of service management philosophies and practices.

The objective of the ITIL Service Management Practices framework is to provide services to business customers that are fit for purpose, stable and which are so reliable that the business views them as a trusted utility.

ITIL Service Management Practices offer best-practice guidance applicable to all types of organizations that provide services to a business. Each publication addresses capabilities having direct impact on a service provider's performance. The structure of the core practice takes form in a service lifecycle. It is iterative and multidimensional. It ensures organizations are set up to leverage capabilities in one area for learning and improvements in others. The core is expected to provide structure, stability and strength to service management capabilities with durable principles, methods and tools. This serves to protect investments and provide the necessary basis for measurement, learning and improvement.

The guidance in the ITIL framework can be adapted for use in various business environments and organizational strategies. The complementary guidance provides flexibility to implement the core in a diverse range of environments. Practitioners can select complementary guidance as needed to provide traction for the core in a given business context, in much the same way as tyres are selected based on the type of automobile, purpose and road conditions. This is to increase the durability and portability of knowledge assets and to protect investments in service management capabilities.

1.2 THE ITIL CORE PRACTICE PUBLICATIONS

The ITIL Service Management Practices comprise three main sets of products and services:

- Core guidance
- Complementary guidance
- Web support services.

1.2.1 ITIL Service Management Practices – core guidance

The core set consists of six publications:

- ■ *The Official Introduction to the ITIL Service Lifecycle*
- ■ *Service Strategy*
- ■ *Service Design*
- ■ *Service Transition*
- ■ *Service Operation*
- ■ *Continual Service Improvement.*

A common structure across all the core guidance publications helps the reader to find references between volumes and to know where to look for similar guidance topics within each stage of the lifecycle.

1.2.2 ITIL Service Management Practices – complementary guidance

This is a living library of publications with guidance specific to industry sectors, organization types, operating models and technology architectures. Each publication supports and enhances the guidance in the ITIL Service Management core. Publications in this category will be continually added to the complementary guidance library and will contain contributions from the expert and user ITSM community. In this way, ITIL Service Management practices are illustrated in real-life situations and in a variety of contexts that add value and knowledge to your own ITIL practice.

1.2.3 ITIL Service Management Practices – web support services

These products are online, interactive services, which will develop over time and include elements such as the glossary of terms and definitions, the interactive service model, online subscriber services, case studies, templates and ITIL Live® – an interactive expert knowledge centre where users can access time with ITSM experts to discuss questions and issues, and seek advice.

Readers of this key element guide are encouraged to explore the entire portfolio of ITIL Service Management publications and services.

1.3 WHAT IS A SERVICE?

Service management is more than just a set of capabilities. It is also a professional practice supported by an extensive body of knowledge, experience and skills. A global community of individuals and organizations in the public and private sectors fosters its growth and maturity. Formal schemes exist for the education, training and certification of practising organizations, and individuals influence its quality. Industry best practices, academic research and formal standards contribute to its intellectual capital and draw from it.

Definition of a service

A service is a means of delivering value to customers by facilitating outcomes customers want to achieve without the ownership of specific costs and risks.

1.4 WHAT IS A LIFECYCLE?

The service lifecycle contains five elements, each of which relies on service principles, processes, roles and performance measures. The ITIL Service Lifecycle uses a hub and spoke design, with Service Strategy at the hub, and Service Design, Transition and Operation as the revolving lifecycle stages, anchored by Continual Service Improvement (Figure 1.1). Each part of the lifecycle exerts influence on the others and relies on the others for inputs and feedback. In this way, a constant set of checks and balances throughout the service lifecycle ensures that as business demand changes with business need, the services can adapt and respond effectively to them.

Figure 1.1 The ITIL Service Lifecycle

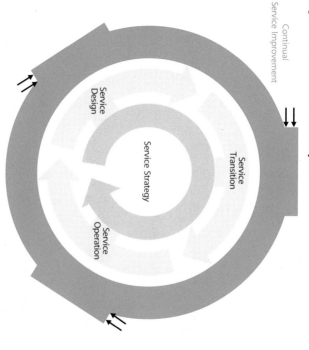

At the heart of the service lifecycle is the key principle – all services must provide measurable value to business objectives and outcomes. ITIL Service Management focuses on business value as its prime objective. Each practice revolves around ensuring that everything a service provider does to manage IT services for the business customer can be measured and quantified in terms of business value. This has become extremely important of late as IT organizations are required to operate as businesses in order to demonstrate a clear return on investment, equating service performance with business value to the customer.

2 The ITIL Service Management Model

The ITIL Service Lifecycle uses models to refine and customize an organization's use of the ITIL Service Management Practices. These models are intended to be reusable in a variety of organizational contexts and to help take advantage of economies of scale and efficiencies.

Central to these models are the overarching process elements that interact throughout the lifecycle and bring power and wisdom to service practices. These service model process elements consist of two main types – lifecycle governance and lifecycle operations. These are depicted in Figure 2.1.

Figure 2.1 Process elements of the ITIL Service Lifecycle

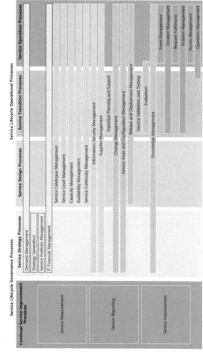

While these processes are non-linear, they do have a logical and sometimes sequential flow. To illustrate this, Figure 2.2 shows the high-level, basic flow of lifecycle process elements in the ITIL Service Lifecycle.

Figure 2.2 A high-level view of the ITIL Service Management Model

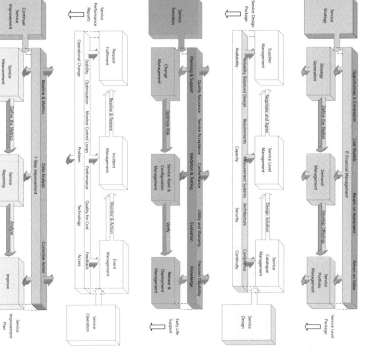

This publication deals with the high-level concepts drawn from the Service Strategy stage of the service lifecycle.

9

3 Principles of Service Strategy

3.1 OBJECTIVES

The primary objective of Service Strategy can be summed up very simply: provide superior performance to competing alternatives. IT service organizations seek to know what customers need (Figure 3.1). After all, every service provider is customer dependent. If the customer does not seek what the organization offers, it will not prosper for long. The organization has two options. It may either make offers to its customers or respond to their requests. Although most organizations do some measure of both, each option requires a fundamentally different approach.

Figure 3.1 Service provider–customer relationships

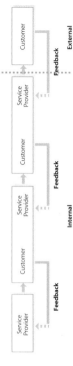

The first approach, called the manufacturing mindset, sees the organization as an efficient factory. Scarcity is a fundamental problem. Whether the constraint is budget, people, floor space or computing capacity, the organization is forever running short on something. Therefore, the more efficiently the organization uses its limited resources, the greater the value it creates. It seeks to lower the unit costs of services by consistently doing the same thing over and over again. Service level agreements (SLAs), for instance, strive for zero defects. Service Desk performance may be based on answering a minimum number of calls on time.

When customer needs are predictable, well established and well defined, the service provider can afford to look inward and focus on 'the one best way'. But customer needs often shift. Customers may encounter increased competition, financial problems, directives to please shareholders or the need to improve their own internal efficiencies. When customer needs become less stable, the service provider may fall into a management trap where internal efficiency is confused with effectiveness or external efficiency. For instance, what is less effective than an engineering team that quickly turns out elegant system designs for the wrong service?

- **Internal efficiency** – the efficient use of production resources; it is also referred to as productivity
- **External efficiency** – the external effectiveness of the service provider as perceived by its customer, also referred to as customer-perceived quality.

It is easy to become confused about what matters to customers and just conduct well-meaning activities focused on 'business as usual – only better'. For example, does the SLA allow the customer to perform better, or are customers frustrated because the IT personnel are more focused on meeting SLA specifications rather than customer success? Does rapid Service Desk response create customer benefits, or does it generate frustration and incomplete work because personnel move too quickly from one call to the next?

The challenge with information-based technologies is that they are seldom perceived as services by IT management, and hence not designed and managed as services to customers. Instead, they are managed as administrative routines with internal efficiency and costs as the main criteria. Consequently, customers see IT as an administrative unit rather than as a service provider. Moving into the role of a service provider is a powerful way of setting apart the IT organization from its competing alternatives.

Internal efficiency is necessary but it is not enough. Customers do not buy services; they buy the satisfaction of particular needs. This means that what the customer values is often different from what the service provider thinks it offers. The more intangible the value, the more important this idea becomes. What counts is quality as it is perceived by customers.

This leads to the second approach, called the marketing mindset. It is an idea that asks the service provider to deliberately search out and capture unarticulated customer needs, cycling quickly through the service lifecycle and converting the customer's desired outcomes into appropriate responses. It means understanding where the organization ought to be headed. And it begins by reaching out to customers and stating, in effect, 'Help me truly understand your needs, and let's work together to satisfy them.'

The challenge is to identify what customers perceive as value. In practice, this is seldom simple or obvious. The value an IT organization seeks to create resides not in its internal abilities and processes but in the customer's perception. Everything the service provider does should flow from that. Value emerges in the customer's consumption or usage of IT services in the pursuit of an outcome for themselves. Only when the service provider comprehends what is effective in creating value is it ready to apply internal efficiency measurements and effect process changes. Long-term success is a matter of identifying the outcomes that matter to the customer and making them visible while making those that are irrelevant either invisible or extinct. A speedier repair process, for example, creates little value if the customer seeks services that never break down. Locking organizational structures, measurement systems, processes and technologies onto customer outcomes, instead of specifications, allows the service provider to better align internal efficiency measurements to external efficiency measurements.

3.2 PRACTICE OF SERVICE STRATEGY

The practice of Service Strategy is intended to aid IT service providers in outperforming competing alternatives over time, across business cycles, industry disruptions and changes in leadership. It comprises both the ability to succeed today and positioning for the future. By understanding the trade-offs involved in its strategic choices, such as services to offer or market spaces to serve, an organization can outperform its competing alternatives and thus satisfy both customers and stakeholders.

The scope of Service Strategy includes guidance for senior managers on how to design, develop and implement service management not only as an organizational capability but also as a strategic asset.

Definition of a strategic asset

A strategic asset is the set of specialized and hard-to-replicate resources and capabilities that create a competitive advantage.

A successful Service Strategy is almost always achieved through the balance, alignment and renewal of three building blocks (Figure 3.2):

■ Market focus and position
■ Distinctive capabilities
■ Performance anatomy.

3.2.1 Market focus and position

These are the 'where and how to compete' aspects of a Service Strategy. High-performance service providers – even internal providers – have great clarity when it comes to setting this strategic direction.

Figure 3.2 Building blocks of high performance

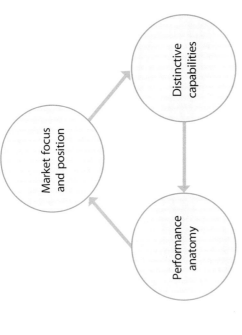

They understand their market spaces, and the customers within, better than their competing alternatives, and manage them through appropriate strategies. Such strategies allow the provider to:

- Build and manage valuable service portfolios
- Achieve optimal scale through sourcing strategies
- Exploit positioning advantages in the value network
- Identify and possibly offer new services
- Better serve customers
- Enter alternative market spaces.

Definition of a value network

A value network is a web of relationships that generates tangible and intangible value through complex dynamic exchanges through two or more organizations.

3.2.2 Distinctive capabilities

This is about creating and exploiting a set of hard-to-replicate capabilities that deliver promised customer outcomes while striving for efficiency. This ability is sometimes referred to as 'differentiation on the outside and simplification on the inside'.

High-performance service providers have great clarity about the resources and capabilities that contribute to facilitating customer outcomes. They understand the need to build capabilities that are demonstrably better and, in the short term, difficult to replicate by competing alternatives. This includes mastering technical capabilities and excelling at innovation, as well as lower cost structures and customer know-how.

3.2.3 Performance anatomy

This comprises a set of organizational 'mindsets' that are measurable and actionable by organizational leadership. These mindsets drive important differences in behaviour – from individual employees to those of the service provider itself – that lead to better customer outcomes. The focus is on creating cultural and organizational characteristics that move the service provider toward its goal of outperforming competing alternatives.

Example mindsets are:

- 'Service management is a strategic asset.'
- 'Workforce productivity is a key execution differentiator.'
- 'Performance measurement is highly selective in its focus and metrics.'

■ 'Continual service improvement and renewal are real and permanent necessities.'

3.3 KEY ELEMENTS

3.3.1 Market spaces

Definition of market spaces

Market spaces are sets of outcomes that customers desire, which can be supported through one or more services.

Harvard marketing professor Theodore Levitt used to tell his students, 'People don't buy a quarter-inch drill. They buy a quarter-inch hole. You've got to study the hole, not the drill. The drill is just a solution for it.' While it is easy to agree with Levitt's insight, it is also easy to focus on the drills instead of the holes. The natural inclination for many IT organizations is to dutifully gather requirements and set to work, offering more and improved features and functions in the belief these will translate into improved customer success. This approach often solves the wrong problems, improving services in ways that are irrelevant to customers' needs. The structure of a market space, seen from the customers' point of view, is very simple. They just need to get things done.

The service provider's challenge is therefore to understand the jobs in customers' lives for which they might use IT services. If IT can understand the job, design a service and associated experiences to facilitate that job or remove constraints, and deliver the service in a way that reinforces its intended use, then when customers find themselves needing to get that job done, they will seek and value that service.

Since IT organizations do not explicitly think in such terms, it becomes easy to focus on capabilities that do not help customers to do their jobs. For this reason, it is useful to think of services in terms of market spaces. A market space represents a set of opportunities for service providers framed in customers' perceived needs or their desired outcomes. Customer relationships are stronger when the provider begins the service lifecycle with a clear understanding of its market spaces.

When service definitions lack clarity about customers' desired outcomes, the expense of the service is difficult to justify. Customers will often express dissatisfaction even when the terms and conditions of SLAs are met. Customers understand and appreciate services only within the context of their own business outcomes, performances and assets. A proper definition of services takes into account the context within which customers perceive value.

The following are simple examples of customer outcomes that can form the basis of one or more market spaces:

- Sales teams are productive with an opportunity management system regardless of location
- Privacy data is monitored and secure
- Loan officers have speedy access to information on loan applicants
- Online billing services offer flexible payment options for shoppers
- Business continuity is assured.

3.3.2 Value creation: utility and warranty

Services create value in many ways, frequently intangible but nonetheless real. The value may take many forms. How useful is it? How reliable is it? What is its quality or reputation? Note that these questions can only be answered by customers. In other words, value is defined by customers, not the service provider.

This understanding begins with simple questions:

- What is our business?
- Who is our customer?
- What does the customer value?
- Who depends on our services?
- How do they use our services?
- Why are our services valuable to them?

The components of value from the customer's perspective may be distilled in this way:

- **Utility** or fitness for purpose
- **Warranty** or fitness for use.

When service requirements are derived from properly understood utility and warranty, the service provider's production operations maintain a stronger linkage with customer outcomes.

Utility articulates the service's desired effect on the customers' outcomes. Utility includes improved performance of associated activities, objects and tasks, as well as the removal or relaxation of constraints on performance (see example in Figure 3.3). Warranty describes the service's positive effect of being available when needed, in sufficient capacity or magnitude, and dependable in terms of continuity and security.

Figure 3.3 Utility map for online check-in service

Productivity	Risk	Convenience	Image	Environmental sustainability
Faster check-in	No loss of tickets	Online transactions/ no standing in line	Improved service encounters	Consume less paper

The terms 'utility' and 'warranty' are not the same as 'functional' and 'non-functional' requirements. Furthering the quarter-inch drill metaphor: utility and warranty describe the hole; functional and non-functional describe the drill.

Consider an IT organization offering a network-based service. When soliciting requirements, the dialogue is often framed in terms meaningful to the service provider, for example response times and availability percentages. The provider then narrows the solution space to these specific criteria within existing internal efficiencies, for example redundant network architectures based on existing T1s and routers.

When customer network services are first framed through desired outcomes – through utility and warranty – new service design options may reveal themselves. For instance, customer outcomes of 'a mobile sales force' and 'unconstrained by location' may now open the solution space to include wireless broadband devices. Once the service provider understands what is important to customers and to what purpose customers use its services, it can look at innovative ways of creating the same or added value without being restricted to providing the service it offered in the past.

3.3.3 Assets, resources and capabilities

An important aspect of service management is the interaction between service assets and customer assets (Figure 3.4).

Service assets

When customers use a service, they are making a choice to avoid certain risks and costs. Some of those decisions are made more thoughtfully than others, but there is always some kind of choice involved. For example, when a business unit decides to run its applications on the IT organization's servers, rather than its own, it is transferring responsibility for the servers' risks and costs to the IT organization. The risks and costs do not go away; someone else takes responsibility for them.

Figure 3.4 Customer and service assets

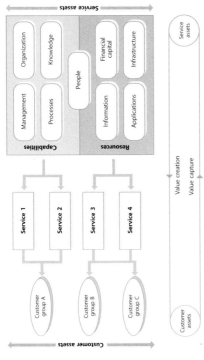

Since the service provider is usually better equipped and specialized to deal with these risks and costs, the decision makes good business sense. In other words, service providers potentially reduce risks and costs for their customers, thereby improving the probability of customer success.

To fulfil this promise, service providers must carefully coordinate and deploy service assets. Service assets are bundles of resources and capabilities owned and managed by the service provider. They are intrinsically different.

- **Resources** – inputs into an organization's operations, such as capital, infrastructure, applications and the skills of individual employees; it is easier to acquire resources than to acquire capabilities

- **Capabilities** – represent an organization's ability to coordinate, control and deploy resources. They are typically experience driven, knowledge intensive, information based and firmly embedded within an organization's people, systems, processes and technologies.

The resources and capabilities underlying production operations differ across organizations. Some are superior to others. What matters is the organization endowed with superior resources and capabilities is better able to satisfy customers or to produce more economically.

Customer assets

While service assets affect the performance of services, services affect the performance of customer assets. Examples of customer assets include employees, business processes, applications, documents and transactions.

Without customer assets there is no basis for defining the value of a service. Therefore the performance of customer assets must be of primary concern to service providers. A service featuring wireless email, for example, increases the performance of one of the most critical of customer assets: managers and staff. Sales managers spend more time on-site with clients, technicians are more quickly dispatched and staff are more easily redistributed.

The impact of a service on customer outcomes is closely tied to its performance impact on customer assets. Some services increase performance, some maintain or restore performance, while others reduce variations in performance.

Without the context of customer assets, the justification for the service cannot be adequately expressed. For example, it is not enough for an internal IT organization to provide market data for an investment bank. The bank's business unit desires improved and reliable trading profits. Hence the data for its traders must be available in real time without interruption during specific trading hours with a contingency plan in place. These are the visible parts of the service that matter to the customer. There may be other fulfilment elements, but, as far as the customer is concerned, the visible activities are to be evaluated in every detail.

The key elements in the above example can be brought together this way: the market space is defined as 'improved and reliable trading profits'. The utility and warranty include productive traders with resilient trading systems. The customer assets are the traders and the trading system. The service assets consist of the real-time market data, highly available infrastructure and the contingency plan. The value of the service is defined by its effect on the customer's assets. The customer is therefore willing to pay a premium for this service over the less expensive data feed.

3.3.4 Types of service provider

Service providers, or service units, can be thought of as a specialized bundle of service assets for delivering services. There are three business model archetypes. A service provider, or the value network for a customer, consists of one or more of the following archetypes.

Type I – internal service provider

A Type I service provider (Figure 3.5) is embedded within a business unit. An enterprise may have more than one Type I service provider.

Figure 3.5 Type I – internal providers

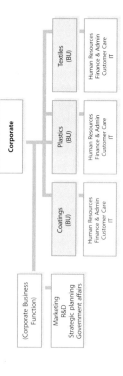

Type II – shared services unit

A Type II service provider (Figure 3.6) is an internal service provider offering shared services to more than one business unit.

Figure 3.6 Type II – shared services

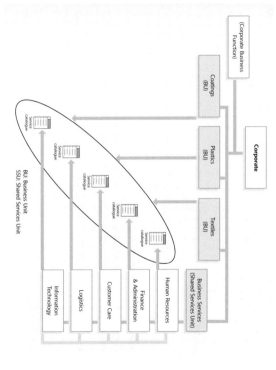

BU: Business Unit
SSU: Shared Services Unit

Type III – external service provider

A Type III service provider (Figure 3.7) is one whose customers are external, i.e. they reside outside the organizational enterprise.

Figure 3.7 Type III – external providers

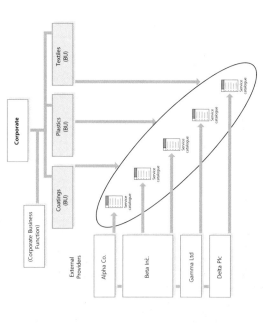

3.3.5 The four Ps

The four Ps (Figure 3.8) correspond to the different forms a Service Strategy may take:

- **Perspective** – this describes a vision and direction. A strategic perspective articulates the business philosophy of interacting with the customer or the manner in which services are provided. For example, a shared service provider for a law firm may adopt the strategic perspective of 'We will be a best-in-class service provider for our law firm'. The CIO determined that their business most values a certain type of service provider.

■ **Position** – this describes the decision to adopt a well-defined stance. Should the provider compete on the basis of value or low cost? Specialized or broad sets of services? Should value be biased towards utility or warranty? An internal service provider restricted to serving one business unit may adopt a position based on 'product know-how' or 'customer responsiveness'. The law firm CIO may adopt a needs-based position: attorney centric offerings for knowledge, collaboration and document management services.

■ **Plan** – this describes the means of transitioning from 'as is' to 'to be'. A plan might detail, 'How do we offer high-value or low-cost services?' Or in the case of the law firm CIO, 'How do we achieve and offer our specialized services?'

■ **Pattern** – this describes a series of consistent decisions and actions over time. A service provider that continually offers specific services with deep expertise is adopting a 'high-value' or 'high-end' Service Strategy. A service provider that continually offers dependable and reliable services is adopting a 'high-warranty' strategy. If mid-course corrections are to be made within the framework of an existing perspective and position, this is where those decisions and actions are formulated. The law firm CIO, for example, may decide to offer the same specialized services but with enhanced levels of client privacy (warranty).

Requirements and conditions are dynamic. A service provider may begin with any one form and evolve to another. For example, a service provider might begin with a perspective: a vision and direction for the organization. It might then decide to adopt a position articulated through policies, resources and capabilities. This position may be achieved through the execution of a carefully crafted plan. Once achieved, the service provider may maintain its position through a series of well-understood decisions and action over time: a pattern.

Figure 3.8 The four Ps in action

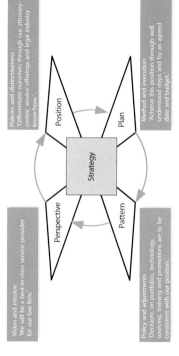

Vision and mission
'We will be a best-in-class service provider
for our law firm.'

Policies and distinctiveness
'Differentiate ourselves through our attorney-
centric service offerings and legal industry
know-how.'

Policy and adjustments
'Decisions on portfolios, technology,
sourcing, training and promotions are to be
consistent with our position.'

Method and execution
'Achieve this position through well
understood steps and by an agreed
date and budget.'

The use of all four Ps, rather than one over the others, allows for
emergent as well as intended service strategies. Best-practice service
strategies mix the four Ps in some way: maintaining control while
fostering learning; seeing the big picture while deciding on details.

3.4 ROLES AND RESPONSIBILITIES

3.4.1 Director of service management and senior IT leaders

Senior leaders of a service provider perform important strategic
responsibilities, which set the foundation for the successful strategic
management of the organization. These responsibilities include:

■ Defining the organization as a service provider
■ Developing and viewing service management as a strategic asset
■ Viewing the organization from a process perspective
■ Managing the value network (suppliers, partnerships and other
relationships) of the Service Portfolio.

3.4.2 Business Relationship Manager

Services are inherently relational. They always lead to some form of cooperation between the service provider and the customer. If the relationship is unsatisfactory, the customer will turn to another service provider. The Business Relationship Manager (BRM) concentrates on managing the customer relationship, including the quality and perceived value. This means that marketing is used to facilitate and support the interactions throughout the relationship, by showing the customer that they are known or valued.

A BRM's internal marketing involves communications management. This is a discrete process for disseminating information about services and promises given to customers. It includes communicating with management about customer needs, views on improving performance and findings of customer wants. It is important that communications management is closely tied with ensuring a customer service mindset (see paragraph 3.4.3).

Gaining insight into the customer's business and having good knowledge of customer outcomes are essential to developing a strong business relationship. BRMs are sometimes known as Account Managers, Business Representatives or Sales Managers. Key responsibilities for BRMs include:

- Seeking direct contact with customers and managing opportunities through a Customer Portfolio
- Building a Customer Portfolio with the necessary information about market spaces, utility and warranty
- Working closely with Product Managers to make it possible to deliver a service offering.

3.4.3 Product Manager

Product Managers take responsibility for developing and managing services across the lifecycle. They are 'product focused' and manage through the Service Portfolio. The role is responsible for managing services as a product over their entire lifecycle, from concept to retirement through design, transition and operation. Product Managers are instrumental in the development of a Service Strategy and its execution through the Service Lifecycle. They are recognized as the subject matter experts on Lines of Service (LOS) and the Service Catalogue. They negotiate internal agreements with BRMs, who represent the needs of customers.

Product Managers work closely with operational staff, engineers, technology specialists and developers when making decisions on how a service evolves over time: when to upgrade a service, what should be in the upgrade, when to retire a service and so on.

A Product Manager's internal marketing involves nurturing a customer service mindset. This is a continual process for managing the attitudes of staff and their motivation for customer outcomes and service management. It is important that attitude management is closely tied with communications management (see paragraph 3.4.2 and Figure 3.9).

Figure 3.9 Product and Relationship Managers

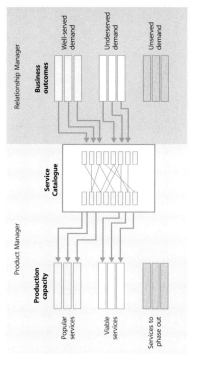

When solutions are not found in the Catalogue or Pipeline, Product Managers and BRMs work together on making a business case for new service development. They involve the Sourcing Management function when there is a need to integrate third-party services and other service components for a new or existing service.

Key responsibilities for Product Managers include:

- Managing service offerings as a product – reducing the mismatch between supply and demand, and industrializing the service operation
- Bringing coordination and focus to the organization around the Service Catalogue
- Working closely with BRMs to make it possible to deliver a service offering.

3.5 SERVICE STRATEGY PROCESSES

3.5.1 Service Strategy generation

The key activities of Service Strategy are Define the Market, Develop the Offerings, Develop Strategic Assets and Prepare for Execution (Figure 3.10).

Figure 3.10 Key activities

Define the market ▷ Develop the offerings ▷ Develop strategic assets ▷ Prepare for execution

Define the market

There are *strategies for services* and *services for strategies*. Strategies for services are the strategies to be developed for the services offered as distinctive capabilities. Services for strategies refer to the management competence for offering services in support of a business strategy.

Defining the market has three elements:

■ **Understand the customer** – the service provider should have an understanding of the kinds of job the customer needs the IT services for. This will facilitate designing the service so that it is fit for the purpose. In this way customers will seek that service when they require it, which gives value to the service

■ **Understand the opportunities** – it is important for service providers to identify explicitly the desired outcomes for every customer and market space that falls within the scope of the particular strategy. Outcomes should be classified and codified with reference tags that can be used across the Service Lifecycle. Customer outcomes that are not well supported may represent opportunities for the service provider

■ **Classify and visualize** – it is useful for managers to classify and visualize service opportunities as value creating patterns. These patterns are made up of customer assets (e.g. information, business process or sales force) and the type of service opportunity (e.g. store, monitor or connect). These classifications and visualizations later form the basis of more formal service definitions of services.

Develop the offerings

Once the market has been defined, the service provider is ready to develop detailed definitions of the service offerings. There are three elements to this activity:

■ **Market space** – a market space represents a set of opportunities for service providers to deliver value to a customer through one or more services. It is at this stage that formal definitions are constructed in terms of customer success. In other words, what does customer success look like? See paragraph 3.3.1 for further details on market spaces.

■ **Outcome-based definitions** – by constructing an outcome-based definition for services to be offered, the service provider ensures that it plans and executes all aspects of service management from the perspective of what is important and valuable to the customer. It is at this stage that utility and warranty are formally constructed. See paragraph 3.3.2 for further details on utility and warranty.

- **Service Portfolio** – the Service Portfolio represents the commitments and investments made by a service provider across all its customers and market spaces. It is at this stage that the service provider begins investing in and committing to service offerings. Service Portfolio is covered in paragraph 3.5.4.

Develop strategic assets

When service providers become adept at helping customers succeed, customers not only value the service, but they are also more inclined to entrust the service provider with additional opportunities, which then further increase the customer's probability of success. In other words, the service provider sets into motion a virtuous cycle benefiting both customer and IT organization. When such a condition exists, service management can be classified as a strategic asset. The service provider possesses a set of specialized and hard-to-replicate resources and capabilities that bestow competitive advantage. This dynamic can be described as a closed-loop control system with the following functions:

- Develop and maintain service assets
- Understand the performance potential of customer assets
- Map service assets to customer assets through services
- Design, develop and operate suitable services
- Extract service potential from service assets
- Convert service potential into performance potential
- Convert demand from customer assets into workload for service assets
- Reduce risks for the customer
- Control the costs of providing services.

Prepare for execution

- Strategic assessment – an established service provider sometimes lacks an understanding of its own unique differentiators. In crafting a Service Strategy, a provider should first take a careful look at what it is doing already, as there probably will be an existing core of differentiation. The following questions can help illuminate a service provider's distinctive capabilities:

– Which of our services or service varieties are the most distinctive? The differentiation can come in the form of barriers to entry, such as the organization's know-how of the customer's business, or the broadness of service offerings. Or the differentiation may be in the form of raised switching costs, due to lower cost structures generated through specialization or service sourcing. It may be a particular attribute not readily found elsewhere, such as product knowledge, regulatory compliance, provisioning speeds, technical capabilities or global support structures.

– Which of our services or service varieties are the most profitable? The form of value may be monetary, as in higher profits or lower expenses, or social, as in saving lives or collecting taxes. For non-profit organizations, are there services that allow the organization to perform its mission better? Substitute 'profit' with 'benefits realized'.

– Which of our customers and stakeholders are the most satisfied?

– Which customers, channels or purchase occasions are the most profitable? Again, the form of value can be monetary, social or other.

– Which of our activities in our value chain or value network are the most different and effective?

Setting objectives – objectives represent the results expected from pursuing strategies, while strategies represent the actions to be taken to accomplish objectives. Clear objectives provide for consistent decision making, minimizing later conflicts. They set forth priorities and serve as standards. To craft its objectives, an organization must understand what outcomes customers desire to achieve and determine how best to satisfy the important outcomes currently underserved. This is how metrics are determined for measuring how well a service is performing. The objectives for a service include three distinct types of data:

- Customer tasks – what activities is the service to carry out? What job is the customer seeking to execute?

- Customer outcomes – what outcomes is the customer attempting to obtain?

- Customer constraints – what constraints may prevent the customer from achieving the desired outcomes? How can the provider remove these constraints?

- Defining critical success factors and competitive analysis – for every market space there are critical success factors that determine the success or failure of a Service Strategy. These factors are influenced by customer needs, business trends, competition, regulatory environment, suppliers, standards, industry best practices and technologies. Critical success factors are also referred to in business literature as strategic industry factors (SIFs).

3.5.2 Demand Management

Poorly managed demand is a source of risk for service providers. Over-provisioning and excess capacity generate costs which customers often look on as waste. Insufficient capacity may impact the quality of services and limit their growth. SLAs, forecasting, planning and tight coordination with the customer can reduce the uncertainty in demand but cannot eliminate it. Also, there is the problem of synchronous production and consumption. Unlike goods, services cannot be stockpiled for later use.

Patterns of business activity

Demand management techniques such as off-peak pricing, volume discounting and differentiated service levels can help shape demand but, ultimately, business activities drive demand for services. As a result, it is important to understand customers' patterns of business activity (PBA). PBA analyses are useful inputs to service management functions and processes:

- Service Catalogue can map demand patterns to appropriate services

- Financial Management can approve suitable incentives to influence demand

- Service Portfolio Management can approve investments in additional capacity, new services or changes to services
- Service Design can optimize designs to suit demand patterns
- Service Operation can adjust allocation of resources and scheduling
- Service Operation can identify opportunities to consolidate demand by grouping closely matching demand patterns.

Core services and supporting services

Core services deliver the basic outcomes desired by the customer. They represent the value that the customer wants and for which they are willing to pay. Supporting services enable the value proposition (Enabling Services or Basic Factors) or improve it (Enhancing Services or Excitement Factors).

Service packages

A service package is a detailed description of an IT service that can be delivered to customers. A service package consists of a service level package (SLP) and one or more core services and supporting services. An SLP is a defined level of utility and warranty for a specific service package. Each SLP is designed to meet the needs of a particular PBA.

SLPs are the genesis of service level requirements, pricing policies and a core service package (CSP). A CSP is a detailed description of a core service that may be shared by two or more SLPs. The advantage of a CSP is that it guarantees strict control of core services used by business units. Every business unit can develop SLPs on the basis of their own applications and processes. CSPs and SLPs can be used in combinations in order to serve customer segments with differentiated values.

3.5.3 Service Portfolio Management

Service Portfolio Management (SPM) is a dynamic method for governing investments in service management across the enterprise and managing them for value.

A Service Portfolio describes a provider's services in terms of business value. It articulates business needs and the provider's response to those needs. By acting as the basis of a decision framework, a Service Portfolio helps to clarify the following strategic questions:

- Why should a customer buy these services?
- Why should they buy these services from us?
- What are the pricing or chargeback models?
- What are our strengths and weaknesses, priorities and risks?
- How should our resources and capabilities be allocated?

Financial Managers tailor a portfolio of investments based on their customer's risk and reward profile. Regardless of the profile, the objective is the same: maximize return at an acceptable risk level. When conditions change, appropriate changes are made to the portfolio. There is a need for applying comparable practices when managing a portfolio of services. The value of a Service Portfolio strategy is demonstrated through the ability to anticipate change while maintaining traceability to strategy and planning. A portfolio is essentially a group of investments that share similar characteristics. They are grouped by size, discipline or strategic value. There are few fundamental differences between IT portfolio management, project portfolio management and SPM. All are enabling techniques for governance. The difference is in the implementation details.

SPM includes the following work methods (Figure 3.11):

- **Define** – specify inventory services, ensure business cases and validate portfolio data
- **Analyse** – maximize portfolio value, align and prioritize, and balance supply and demand
- **Approve** – finalize proposed portfolio, and authorize services and resources
- **Charter** – communicate decisions, allocate resources and charter services.

Figure 3.11 Service Portfolio Management

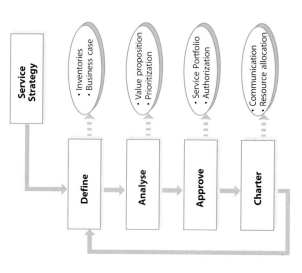

Define

In this step information is collected from all existing services as well as every proposed service. Every proposed service includes those in a conceptual phase, i.e. all services the organization would do if it had unlimited resources, capabilities and time. This documentation exercise is done to better understand the opportunity costs of the existing portfolio. If a service provider understands what it cannot do, then it is better able to assess whether it should keep doing what it is doing or reallocate its resources and capabilities.

The next step in the process set, Analyse, should be well defined before beginning the Define phase. If the organization does not understand what analysis it will perform, it is unlikely to know the right data to collect. Data collection exercises are usually disruptive and should be as streamlined as possible. The cyclic nature of SPM means that this phase not only creates an initial inventory of services, but it also validates the data on a recurring basis. Different portfolios will have different refresh cycles. Some cycles will be triggered by a particular event or business trend. For example, a Merger and Acquisition may trigger a portfolio re-evaluation.

Every service in the portfolio should include a business case. A business case is a model of what a service is expected to achieve. It is the justification for pursuing a course of action to meet stated organizational goals. As such, it acts as the link back to Service Strategy and funding. It is the assessment of a service investment in terms of potential benefits and the resources and capabilities required to provision and maintain it.

Analyse

This is where strategic intent is crafted. It begins with a set of top-down questions:

■ What are the long-term goals of the service organization?
■ What services are required to meet those goals?
■ What capabilities and resources are required for the organization to achieve those services?
■ How will we get there?

In other words, what are the perspective, position, plan and pattern? The answers to these questions guide not only the analysis but also the desired outcomes of SPM. The ability to satisfactorily answer these questions requires the involvement of senior leaders and subject matter experts. See paragraph 3.3.5.

Approve

The previous phases have led to a well-understood future state ('to be'). This is where deliberate approvals or disapprovals of that future state take place. With approval comes the corresponding authorization for new services and resources. The disposition for existing services falls into six categories:

- Retain – largely self-contained, with well-defined asset, process and system boundaries, these services are aligned with and are relevant to the organization's strategy

- Replace – these services have unclear and overlapping business functionality

- Rationalize – these services are composed of multiple releases of the same operating system, multiple versions of the same software and/or multiple versions of system platforms providing similar functions

- Re-engineer – these services meet the technical and functional criteria of the organization but display unclear process or system boundaries. An example would be a service handling its own authentication or continuity functions. In such cases, the service can often be re-engineered to include only the core functionality, with common services used to provide the remainder. Re-engineering is also useful when a service embeds potentially reusable business services within itself

- Renew – these services meet functional fitness criteria but fail technical fitness. An example would be a service whose fulfilment elements include a frame relay network where the strategic direction of the organization is to source an MPLS (Multi-Protocol Label Switching) WAN

- Retire – these services do not meet minimum levels of technical and functional fitness.

Charter

Begin with a list of decisions and action items. These are to be communicated to the organization clearly and unambiguously. These decisions are correlated to budgetary decisions and financial plans. Budget allocations should enforce the allocation of resources. The expected value of each

3.5.4 Service Portfolio

The Service Portfolio represents the commitments and investments made by a service provider across all its customers and market spaces. It represents present contractual commitments, new service development, and ongoing service improvement programmes initiated by Continual Service Improvement. The portfolio also includes third-party services, which are an integral part of service offerings to customers. Some third-party services are visible to the customers whereas others are not.

Portfolios instil a certain financial discipline necessary to avoid making investments that will not yield value. Service Portfolios represent the ability and readiness of a service provider to serve its customers and market spaces. The Service Portfolio is divided into three phases: Service Pipeline, Service Catalogue and Retired services (Figure 3.12).

Service Pipeline

The Service Pipeline consists of services under development for a given customer or market space. These services are phased into operation by Service Transition after completion of design, development and testing. The pipeline represents the service provider's growth and strategic outlook for the future. It also reflects the extent to which new service concepts and ideas for improvement are being fed by Service Strategy, Service Design and Continual Service Improvement. Sound financial management is necessary to ensure adequate funding for the pipeline.

service should be built into financial forecasts and resource plans. Tracking both tracks the progress of service investments. Newly chartered services are promoted to Service Design. Existing services are refreshed in the Service Catalogue. Retired services begin their sunset to Service Transition.

Figure 3.12 Service Pipeline and Service Catalogue

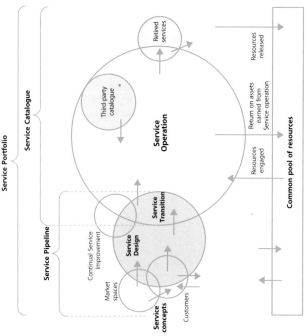

Area of circle is proportional to resources currently engaged in the lifecycle phase (Service Portfolio and Financial Management)

Service Catalogue

The Service Catalogue is the subset of the Service Portfolio visible to customers. It consists of services presently active in the Service Operation phase and those approved to be readily offered to current or prospective customers. It is an expression of the service provider's operational capabilities within the context of a customer or market space.

The Service Catalogue serves as a service order and demand channelling mechanism. It communicates and defines the policies, guidelines and accountability required for SPM. It defines the criteria for what services fall under SPM and the objective of each service. It acts as the acquisition portal for customers, including pricing and service level commitments, and the terms and conditions for service provisioning. It is in the Service Catalogue that services are decomposed into components; where assets, processes and systems are introduced with entry points and terms for their use and provisioning. As providers may have many customers or serve many businesses, there may be multiple Service Catalogues projected from the Service Portfolio.

Retired services

There is sometimes a need to retire or withdraw a service offering. This activity occurs during the Service Transition phase. This is to ensure that all commitments made to customers are duly fulfilled and service assets are released from contracts. When services are phased out, the related knowledge and information are stored in a knowledge base for future use. Retired services are not available to new customers or contracts unless a special business case or alternative provisions are made. Such services may be reactivated into operations under special conditions and SLAs that need to be approved by senior management.

3.5.5 Financial Management

Financial Management as a strategic tool is applicable to all three service provider types. Internal service providers are increasingly asked to operate with the same levels of financial visibility and accountability as their business unit and external counterparts. Moreover, technology and innovation have become core revenue-generating capabilities for many companies. Financial Management provides the business and IT with the financial quantification of the value of IT services, the value of the assets underlying the provisioning of those services, and the qualification of operational forecasting.

Service Valuation

Service Valuation financially quantifies the funding sought by the business and IT for services delivered, based on the agreed value of those services.

The pricing of a service is the cost-to-value translation necessary to achieve clarity and influence the demand and consumption of services. The activity involves identifying the cost baseline for services and then quantifying the perceived value added by a provider's service assets in order to conclude a final service value. The primary goal of Service Valuation is to produce a value for services that the business perceives as fair, and fulfils the needs of the provider in terms of supporting it as an ongoing concern. A secondary objective is the improved management of demand and consumption behaviour. Service valuation focuses primarily on two key valuation concepts:

- Provisioning Value
- Service Value Potential.

Provisioning Value is the underlying cost to IT related to provisioning a service, including all fulfilment elements, both tangible and intangible. Input comes from financial systems, and consists of payment for actual resources consumed in the provisioning of a service. Cost elements include items such as:

- Hardware and software licence costs
- Annual maintenance fees for hardware and software
- Personnel resources used in the support or maintenance of a service
- Utilities, data centre or other facilities charges
- Taxes, capital or interest charges
- Compliance costs.

The sum of these actual service costs represents the baseline from which the minimum value of a service is calculated since providers are seldom willing to offer a service where they are unable to recover the provisioning cost. Of course there are exceptions to this, especially related to Type I providers in situations where alternatives for provisioning of a specific service are limited or non-existent.

Service Value Potential is the value-added component derived from the customer's perception of value from the service or expected marginal utility and warranty from using the service. Provisioning Value elements add up first to establish a baseline. The value-added components of the service are then monetized individually according to their perceived value to estimate the true value of the service package. These components are then summed along with the baseline costs to determine the value of the service.

Demand modelling

Poorly managed service demand is a source of cost and risk. The tight coupling of service demand and capacity (consumption and production) requires Financial Management to quantify funding variations resulting from changes in service demand. Financial demand modelling focuses on identifying the total cost of utilization (TCU) to the customer, and predicting the financial implications of future service demand.

Inputs for managing service demand include pricing and incentive adjustments intended to alter customer consumption patterns. This is not possible without demand data from Capacity Management and the Service Catalogue, translated into financial requirements. Service demand planning is translated to financial funding requirements for the entire enterprise at a business unit level or lower, and consumption of both services and budgets can be viewed in real time through an extension of the Service Catalogue.

Through the application of Financial Management, the Service Catalogue provides customers with the capability to regulate their demand and prepare budgets. This partially addresses the problem of over-consumption. Capacity planning also provides important information related to service demand by providing usage data and trend reporting from a technical component perspective.

Service Portfolio Management

Financial Management is a key input to SPM. By understanding cost structures applied in the provisioning of a service, a company can benchmark service costs against other providers. Organizations can then use financial information, together with service demand and internal capability information, to make sourcing decisions.

Service Provisioning Optimization

Financial Management provides key inputs for Service Provisioning Optimization (SPO). SPO examines the financial inputs and constraints of service components or delivery models to determine if alternatives should be explored. A typical candidate for this type of examination includes services identified for removal from the Service Portfolio because they can no longer be provisioned efficiently relative to other providers or service alternatives, or they experience declining usage due to factors such as obsolescence.

Planning confidence

One goal of Financial Management is to ensure proper funding for the delivery and consumption of services. Planning provides financial translation and qualification of expected future demand for IT services. Financial Management Planning focuses on demand and supply variances resulting from business strategy, capacity inputs and forecasting rather than traditional individual line item expenditures or business cost accounts. Planning can be categorized into three main areas, each representing financial results that are required for continued visibility and service valuation:

- Operating and Capital (general and fixed asset ledgers)
- Demand (need and use of IT services – discussed earlier in this chapter)
- Regulatory and Environmental (compliance).

Service investment analysis

The objective of service investment analysis is to derive a value indication for the total lifecycle of a service based on the value received, and costs incurred during the lifecycle of the service.

Financial Management provides the shared analytical models and knowledge used throughout an enterprise in order to assess the expected value and/or return of a given initiative, solution, programme or project in a standardized fashion. It sets the thresholds that guide the organization in determining what level of analytical sophistication is to be applied to various projects based on size, scope, resources, cost and related parameters.

Accounting

Accounting within Financial Management differs from traditional accounting in that additional categories and characteristics must be defined that enable the identification and tracking of service-oriented expense or capital items.

Financial Management has a translational role between corporate financial systems and service management. The result of a service-oriented accounting function is that far greater detail and understanding is achieved regarding service provisioning and consumption, and the generation of data that feeds directly into the planning process. The functions and accounting characteristics that come into play are:

■ Service recording – the assignment of a cost entry to the appropriate service. Depending on how services are defined, and the granularity of the definitions, there may be additional sub-service components.

■ Cost Types – these are higher-level expenses categories such as hardware, software, labour, administration, etc. These attributes assist with reporting and analysing demand and usage of services and their components in commonly used financial terms.

- Cost classifications – there are classifications within services that designate the end purpose of the cost. These include classifications such as:
    - Capital/operational
    - Direct/indirect
    - Fixed/variable
    - Cost Units.

Compliance

Compliance is the ability to demonstrate that proper and consistent accounting methods and/or practices are being employed. This relates to financial asset valuation, capitalization practices, revenue recognition, access and security controls etc.

The implementation of public frameworks and standards such as COBIT, ISO/IEC 20000, Basel II and other industry-specific regulation may appear to be pure costs with no tangible benefits. However, regulatory compliance tends to improve data security and quality processes, creating a greater need for understanding the costs of compliance. Services provisioned in one industry at a certain price may not necessarily be provisioned at the same price to a different industry segment. There are instances where the cost of compliance has been large enough to have an impact on the pricing of a service.

Variable Cost Dynamics

Variable Cost Dynamics (VCD) focuses on analysing and understanding the variables that impact service cost, how sensitive those elements are to variability and the related incremental value changes that result. VCD analysis can be used to identify a marginal change in unit cost resulting from adding or subtracting one or more incremental units of a service. Such an analysis is helpful when applied toward the analysis of expected impacts from events such as acquisitions, divestitures, changes to the Service Portfolio or service provisioning alternatives. Below is a subset of possible variable service cost components involved in such an analysis:

- Number and type of users
- Number of software licences
- Cost/operating footprint of data centre
- The cost of adding one more storage device
- The cost of adding one more end-user licence.

Return on investment

Return on investment (ROI) is a concept for quantifying the value of an investment. In service management, ROI is used as a measure of the ability to use assets to generate additional value. This covers three areas:

- Business case – a means to identify business imperatives that depend on service management
- Pre-Programme ROI – techniques for quantitatively analysing an investment in service management
- Post-Programme ROI – techniques for retroactively analysing an investment in service management.

3.6   STRATEGY AND ORGANIZATION

Outside forces greatly influence an organization's Service Strategy, which in turn determines the organizational structure. Where the lines are drawn depends on what the organization is attempting to accomplish. A Service Strategy then becomes an implicit blueprint for an organization's design, shaping scale and scope. Scale refers to size. Scope refers not only to the broadness of service offerings, but it also describes the range of activities the organization performs. As the organization grows and matures, changes in roles and relationships must be made or problems will arise. This is particularly important for organizations adopting a service orientation, as pressures for efficiency and discipline inevitably lead to greater formalization and complexity.

Organizations are generally characterized by a dominant management style: Network, Directive, Delegative, Coordinated or Collaborative. Each style serves the needs of the organization for a period of time. As service requirements evolve, the organization encounters a dominant management challenge that must be resolved before growth can continue. The organization can no longer address its service challenge with its current management style.

3.6.1 Network

The focus of a Network organization (Figure 3.13) is on the rapid, informal and ad hoc delivery of services. The organization is highly technology oriented, perhaps entrepreneurial and is reluctant to adopt formal structures. Innovation and entrepreneurship are important organizational values. The organization learns which processes and services work and adjusts accordingly.

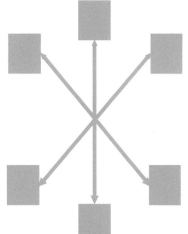

Figure 3.13 Network management style

3.6.2 Directive

The focus of a directive organization is on hierarchical structures that separate functional activities. Communication is more formal and basic processes are in place. Although effort and energy are diligently applied to services, they are likely to be inefficient. Functional specialists are frequently faced with the difficult decision of whether to follow the process or take the initiative on their own.

3.6.3 Delegative

The focus of a delegative organization (Figure 3.14, left panel) is on the proper application of a decentralized organizational structure. More responsibility shifts from functional owners to process owners. Process owners focus on process improvement and customer responsiveness. The challenge is when functional and process objectives clash.

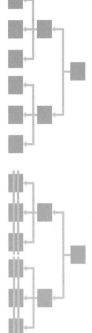

Figure 3.14 Delegative and coordinated management

3.6.4 Coordinated

The focus of a coordinated organization (Figures 3.14 and 3.15) is on the use of formal systems in achieving greater coordination. Senior executives acknowledge the criticality of these systems and take responsibility for success of the solutions. The solutions lead to planned service management structures that are intensely reviewed and continually improved. Each service is treated as a carefully nurtured and monitored investment. Technical functions remain centralized while service management processes are decentralized.

Figure 3.15 Coordinated and collaborative management

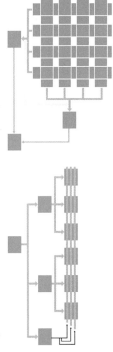

3.6.5 Collaborative

The focus here is on stronger collaboration with the business. Relationship management is more flexible, while managers are highly skilled in teamwork and conflict resolution. The organization responds to changes in business conditions and strategy in the form of teams across functions. Experiments in new practices are encouraged. A matrix-type structure is frequently adopted in this phase. A matrix structure is a rectangular grid that shows the vertical flow of functional responsibility and a horizontal flow of product or customer responsibility (Figure 3.15). The provider effectively has two (or more) line organizations, each with separate lines of authority and a balance of power; two (or more) bosses, each actively participating in strategy setting and governance.

3.7 TECHNOLOGY AND STRATEGY

3.7.1 Service automation

Automation can have particularly significant impact on the performance of service assets such as management, organization, people, process, knowledge and information. Automation is a means to industrialize the utility and warranty of services, and offers several advantages:

- The capacity of automated resources can be more easily adjusted in response to variations in demand volumes

- Automated resources can handle capacity with fewer restrictions on time of access; they can therefore be used to serve demand across time zones and outside normal working hours

- Automated systems present a good basis for measuring and improving service processes by holding constant the factor of human resources

- Many optimization problems such as scheduling, routing and allocation of resources require computing power that is beyond the capacity of human agents

- Automation is a means for capturing the knowledge required for a service process. Codified knowledge is relatively easy to distribute throughout the organization in a consistent and secure manner.

The following are some of the areas where service management can benefit from automation:

- Design and modelling
- Service Catalogue
- Pattern recognition and analysis
- Classification, prioritization and routing
- Detection and monitoring
- Optimization.

3.7.2 Preparing for automation

Automation should not be applied indiscriminately. The following guidelines should be followed:

- Simplify the service processes before automating them
- Clarify the flow of activities, allocation of tasks, need for information and interactions
- In self-service situations, reduce the surface area of the contact the users have with the underlying systems and processes
- Do not be in a hurry to automate tasks and interactions that are neither simple nor routine in terms of inputs, resources and outcomes.

3.7.3 Types of service technology encounters

Advances in communication technologies are having a profound effect on the manner in which service providers interact with customers. Airport kiosks, for example, have changed the interaction between airlines and their customers. There are five modes in which technology interacts with a service provider's customers (Figure 3.16):

- **Mode A, technology-free** – technology is not involved in the service encounter; consulting services, for example, may be Mode A
- **Mode B, technology-assisted** – a service encounter where only the service provider has access to the technology, e.g. an airline representative who uses a terminal to check in passengers is Mode B
- **Mode C, technology-facilitated** – a service encounter where both the service provider and the customer have access to the same technology, e.g. a planner in consultation with a customer can refer to 'what if' scenarios on a personal computer to illustrate capacity and availability modelling profiles
- **Mode D, technology-mediated** – a service encounter where the service provider and the customer are not in physical proximity; communication may be through a phone, e.g. a customer who receives technical support services from a Service Desk is Mode D
- **Mode E, technology-generated** – a service encounter where the service provider is represented entirely by technology, commonly known as self-service, e.g. bank ATMs, online banking and distance learning are Mode E.

Figure 3.16 Types of service encounter

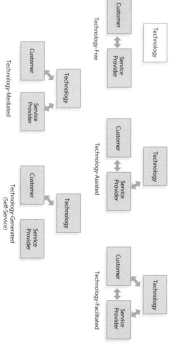

Technology-Free

Customer ↔ Service Provider

Technology-Mediated

Customer ↔ Technology ↔ Service Provider

Technology-Assisted

Customer | Technology ↔ Service Provider

Technology-Generated (Self-Service)

Customer ↔ Technology | Service Provider

Technology-Facilitated

Customer ↔ Technology | Service Provider

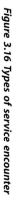

Encounters should be designed bearing in mind customer assets.

- Are the customer's employees technical or non-technical!?
- What are the implications of the technology encounter for the customer?
- What are the customer's expectations and perceptions? For example, Mode E may be less effective than Mode B or Mode C in cases where the encounter is complex or ambiguous. When the encounter is routine and explicit, as in password resets, Mode E may be preferred. Other modes may have secondary considerations. Mode D, for example, may have language or time-zone implications.

3.8   RISKS

Risk is defined as the uncertainty of outcome, positive or negative. While services reduce risks to the customer's business, they also transfer risk to the service provider. For example, by maintaining and operating service assets (e.g. staff, facilities or server) so that customers do not have to, the service provider is assuming risks associated with those assets (e.g. staff attrition, facility security or server malfunction).

The burden of risks can be accounted for in the pricing of services. When this is not possible, providers should engage their customers in dialogue on compensation for risks within the framework of corporate policy. When it is not possible to account for the burden of risks in pricing of services, it should nevertheless be explicitly highlighted for the customer.

Risk analysis and risk management should be applied to the Service Pipeline and Service Catalogue to identify and mitigate risks within the Service Lifecycle. In this context:

- Risk analysis is concerned with gathering information about exposure to risk so that the organization can make appropriate decisions and manage the risk appropriately

- Risk management involves having processes in place to monitor risks, provide access to reliable and up-to-date information about risks, maintain the right balance of control for dealing with those risks and enable decision-making processes supported by a framework of risk analysis and evaluation.

3.8.1 Service provider risks

Risks materialize in various forms, such as technical problems, loss of control in operations, breaches in information security, delays in launching services, failure to comply with regulations and financial shortfalls. The exposure to risks and resulting damages can be measured financially and in terms of the loss of goodwill among customers, suppliers and partners.

3.8.2 Contract risks

Customers depend on contracts as a means of allocating and managing most, if not all, operational risks associated with their business outcomes. The concept of 'contract' includes formal, legally binding contracts as well as less formal agreements between business units and internal groups and functions. Risks that threaten the ability of the service provider to deliver on contractual commitments are strategic risks because they jeopardize not only operations in the present but also the confidence customers will place in the provider in future.

3.8.3 Design and operational risks

Risks are associated with contracts and span the Service Lifecycle. They are identified and assigned to roles and responsibilities within the functions and processes of the lifecycle. The set of risks to be managed depends on the commitments contained in the Contract Portfolio, which define the design requirements and the operational requirements to be realized through Service Models and Service Operation Plans. The combination of the two complementary sets of requirements determines the risks to be managed.

Service Transition is instrumental in identifying risks in contractual commitments. The risk management is applied from the period before the commitments are made, through Service Design, and until the commitments are fulfilled through Service Operation. Design risks arise from the failures or shortcomings in converting requirements into proper services and service models. Operational risks arise from technical and administrative failures in supporting the service model in operation. Together they determine the larger set of risks to be managed actively across the Service Lifecycle.

3.9   KEY MESSAGES AND LESSONS

■ See the IT organization through the eyes of its customer. No organization acts in a vacuum. Customers always have alternatives – even for government and not-for-profit organizations, where alternative social services compete for scarce tax revenues and contributions. Competitive forces demand that an IT organization should do its job better than th ese alternatives. It means be ng different – either in the services you provide or how you provide them. It may be in the form of lower cost structures or service quality. Or it may be in the form of customer or produc t know-how. Either way, it is a distinctiveness not easily found elsewhere. Every IT organization, regardless of whether it is internal or external, commercial or not-for-profit, has the imperative of taking a service perspective and adopting a Service Strategy. Service Strategy need not simply be an exercise in gathering requirements or the pursuit of operational effectiveness. It is a means to become not optional.

■ Success in Service Strategy depends on identifying what customers perceive as value. The value an IT organization seeks to create resides not in its internal abilities but in the customer's perception. Everything else a service provider does should flow from that.

■ Long-term success is a matter of identifying the outcomes that matter to the customer and making them visible while making those that are irrelevant either invisible or extinct. Locking organizational structures, measurement systems, processes and technologies onto customer outcomes allow the service provider to better serve its customers.

■ By understanding the trade-offs involved in its strategic choices, such as services to offer or market spaces to serve, an organization can better outperform its competing alternatives and thus satisfy both customers and stakeholders. A successful Service Strategy is almost always achieved through the balance, alignment and renewal of three building blocks: market focus and position, distinctive capabilities and performance anatomy.

4   Further guidance and contact points

Other frameworks or methodologies that have valid contributions to make to Service Strategy and have synergy with ITIL are listed below.

Programme and project management

Many organizations adopt programme and project management methodologies and frameworks to manage business and technology change. Further guidance on these topics includes:

■ *Managing Successful Programmes*, Office of Government Commerce, 2007 (The Stationery Office, Norwich)

ISBN-13: 978-0113310401

■ *Managing Successful Projects with PRINCE2*, Office of Government Commerce, 2007 (The Stationery Office, Norwich)

ISBN-13: 978-0113309467

■ *A Guide to the Project Management Body of Knowledge* (PMBOK® Guides), 3rd edn, Project Management Institute, 2004 (Project Management Institute, Pennsylvania)

ISBN-13: 978-1930699458.

Visit www.prince-officialsite.com for more information on project management using PRINCE2™, and www.pmi.org for more information on project management, PMI and PMBOK.

Service management

■ Haeckel, Stephan, 1999. *Adaptive Enterprise: Creating and Leading Sense-And-Respond Organizations*. Harvard Business School Press

■ Gronroos, Christian, 2007. *Service Management and Marketing: Customer Management in Service Competition*. 3rd edn. John Wiley and Sons.

Management of Risk

Management of Risk (M_o_R®) is a framework and standard methodology for the management of risk. It provides guidance on the principles, the approach and the processes that should be used in the management of risk within an organization. See:

- Office of Government Commerce, 2007. *Management of Risk: Guidance for Practitioners*, TSO

  ISBN-13: 978-0113310388.

Service oriented architecture

The service oriented architecture (SOA) approach is used by many organizations to improve their effectiveness and efficiency in the provision of IT services. SOA brings value and agility to an organization by encouraging the development of 'self-contained' services that are reusable, promoting a flexible approach to the development of 'shared services'. The structures within SOA can help in designing configuration models and the Configuration Management System.

Control Objectives for Information and related Technology

The Control Objectives for Information and related Technology (COBIT) framework, from the IT Governance Institute (ITGI), provides a framework of guidance for IT audit and security personnel.

The current version of COBIT, edition 4, includes 34 High Level Control Objectives, 10 of which are grouped under the 'Plan and Organise Domain' and seven within 'Acquire and Implement Domain'. Visit www.itgi.org for more information on COBIT.

Quality management

There are distinct advantages of implementing service management within an organization as part of its quality management system. If an organization has a formal quality management system, such as

ISO9000, Six Sigma, Total Quality Management (TQM), etc., then this can be used to assess progress regularly and drive forward agreed service improvement initiatives through regular reviews and reporting.

For more information on Six Sigma, visit www.ge.com/sixsigma/makingcustomers.html or source one of the following:

- Peter S. Pande, Robert P. Neuman and Roland R. Cavanagh, 2000. *The Six Sigma Way: How GE, Motorola, and Other Top Companies are Honing Their Performance*, McGraw-Hill

  ISBN-13: 978-0071358064

- Pete Pande and Larry Holpp, 2001. *What Is Six Sigma?*, McGraw-Hill

  ISBN-13: 978-0071381857

- Michael L. George, 2003. *Lean Six Sigma for Service: How to Use Lean Speed and Six Sigma Quality to Improve Services and Transactions*, McGraw-Hill

  ISBN-13: 978-0071418218.

ISO/IEC 20000

Organizations can seek independent accreditation against the International Organization for Standardization standard ISO/IEC 20000. This standard is supported by a series of publications from the British Standards Institution (BSI) titled 'Achieving ISO/IEC 20000'.

ISO/IEC 20000 initially mapped to the prior *Service Support* and *Service Delivery* publications of ITIL. It continues to map well to ITIL Service Management Practices today and many organizations use the ITIL Service Lifecycle to help them to achieve the standard.

Visit www.iso.org for more information on:

- ISO/IEC 20000 Information Technology Service Management
- ISO/IEC 27001 Information technology – Security techniques Information Security Management Systems

- ISO/IEC 17799 Information technology – Security techniques Code of practice for Information Security Management
- ISO/IEC 19770 Information technology – Software asset management Part 1: Processes
- ISO/IEC 15504 Information technology – Process assessment.

Capability Maturity Model Integration

The Capability Maturity Model® Integration (CMMI) is a process improvement approach developed by the Software Engineering Institute (SEI) of Carnegie Mellon University in Philadelphia. CMMI helps integrate traditionally separate organizational functions and set process improvement goals and priorities, and provides guidance for quality processes and a point of reference for appraising current processes.

Visit www.sei.cmu.edu/cmmi for more information on CMMI.

Balanced Scorecard

The Balanced Scorecard provides a clear prescription as to what companies should measure in order to 'balance' various perspectives:

- Learning and Growth
- Business Process
- Customer
- Financial.

ITIL Service Management Practices

Visit www.itil-officialsite.com for more information on all things ITIL.

- Office of Government Commerce, 2007. *Service Strategy*, TSO

  ISBN-13: 978-0113310456

- Office of Government Commerce, 2007. *Service Design*, TSO

  ISBN-13: 978-0113310470

- Office of Government Commerce, 2007. *Service Transition*, TSO

  ISBN-13: 978-0113310487

- Office of Government Commerce, 2007. *Service Operation*, TSO

  ISBN-13: 978-0113310463

- Office of Government Commerce, 2007. *The Official Introduction to the ITIL Service Lifecycle*, TSO

  ISBN-13: 978-0113310616.

Visit www.ogc.gov.uk for more information on the Office of Government Commerce, which owns the ITIL copyright.

Visit www.tso.co.uk for more information on TSO (The Stationery Office), which publishes the ITIL volumes, and www.best-management-practice.com.

Visit www.apmgroup.co.uk for more information on APMG, the accreditor of ITIL certifications.